Securing The Home

Keys For Home Security

And Personal Protection

Bobby Ricks, CPP   Jeffrey Dingle, CPP

Securing The Home

Published by:
Bolivar Publishing
Berea, Kentucky

ISBN 13: 978-0-9976489-0-4

Graphics:
Images used under license from Shutterstock.com

Disclaimer: The information in this book is non inclusive and should not be used as a substitute for a professional security survey. While products and services are mentioned, this does not in any way constitute an endorsement of the product or service; use your own judgment in choosing products or services.

Table of Contents

Appendices

Introduction:

We wrote this book for the family. For many, this is the start to becoming proactive in family safety. The book is packed with suggestions to improve the security of your family and your home. Use it as a source book for assessing your needs and making decisions.

Most security books are technical and written for the security practitioner. We have published such a book.[1] But, we saw a need to write a book that covers common concerns of home and personal safety. Our objective is to get families thinking with security and safety in mind.

As Certified Protection Professionals®, we took our combined experience of over sixty years in the security field and focused on the home. Now, take this experience and feel safe, be safe, and secure.

Bobby Ricks
Jeff Dingle

---

[1] Ricks, Ricks and Dingle 2014, *Physical Security and Safety: A Field Guide for the Practitioner,* CRC Press

Key 1 - Doors and Windows

We begin by looking at doors and windows, the most common points of entry into a home. This Key looks at how you get in and out of your home, and how you keep others from getting in and out.

Doors

Make sure all of your doors and windows are in good repair. Doors and windows should close completely and securely latch when the doors and windows are closed.

Exterior doors should be make of solid wood or metal at least 1 ¾ inch thick. They should be strong enough to prevent an intruder from kicking through the door. Good locks don't offer much protection on weak doors. Make sure there are no screws missing from the hinges, and make sure the door knobs are in good working order.

Quality door locks are a necessity and door locks are easily replaced. It is recommended that exterior doors have deadbolt locks, with at least a one inch bolt. Both the face plate (the metal part around the bolt on the side of the door) and the strike plate (the metal piece that the bolt goes into on the door frame) should have screws at least an inch and a half holding the strike plate in place. Ideally, the screws should be long enough to extend beyond the door frame and into the building frame. This keeps the door and lock intact in the event that someone tries to force the door open.

A product that has been successful in preventing doors being kicked is the Jamb Enforcer. This tool is a 48"steel insert that installs inside the door frame and secures the frame to the building studs with long screws.

If you have a garage, ALWAYS lock the door between the garage and the home. Many people feel that a closed garage is sufficient to keep an intruder out, but it is not. ALWAYS keep that door locked.

Windows

Windows must lock securely. Many windows have built in stops to allow a window to be left open a little, not opened enough to allow a person to crawl through. Windows without a built in stop can be pinned for security. Pinning is accomplished by drilling a 3/16" hole on a slight downward slant through the inside window frame and halfway into the outside frame. Place a nail in the hole to secure the window.

When you leave your home, close and lock the windows, even the small bathroom window that you think nobody could possibly fit through

Increase security by planting rosebushes or cactus type plants or shrubs in front of all vulnerable windows. Thorny landscaping not only adds beauty to your home, but makes even getting close to these windows an unappealing prospect.

Blinds or curtains should be used to prevent visibility into your home, especially when you are not at home. Window film is an option that adds multiple benefits. Products such as ShatterGard® are a film you apply to the window glass that holds glass together when attacked. The film also offers UV protection, and can be clear or tinted. Film the most vulnerable windows, usually the lower level windows.

Last – your doors have locks, use them! The most common way a burglar enters a home is through an unlocked door. It is a good practice to keep all of your doors locked, even when you are home.

4 Ricks & Dingle

Key 2 - The Yard.

Your yard forms the perimeter around your home. Look at your yard, and make sure that anything that can be used against you is put away. Ladders left unsecured can be used to access second floor windows. Tools (hammers, wrenches) left out can be stolen, or be used to break windows. Make sure ladders or anything that someone could use to stand on are put away or locked up.

Look at what is growing in your yard. Bushes and shrubs should be kept trimmed low so a person is unable to hide behind them. This is not to say you shouldn't have bushes and shrubs in your yard, just make sure they don't cover points of entry like windows and doors. Flowers are perfect, and trees should be where they are not blocking the view of your exterior doors. You should have a good, unobstructed view of the doors on the front of your home from your driveway.

There are several issues to consider if you have a fence. A fence that you can see through, such as a chain link fence, offers several positive issues. A chain link fence keeps children and animals in, keeps other children and animals out, and provides a level of security for your back yard. However, solid fences, such as board, shadowbox or PVC fences provide the same purpose as a chain link fence, they also provide privacy. The problem is that they also provide privacy for an intruder or a burglar. Remember, if you can't see into your backyard, your neighbors and the police can't see if there is someone in your backyard either!

Gates need to be closed and locked and secured when not in use. While almost anyone can climb a fence, making it just a *little bit* more difficult will often deter an intruder. A "Beware of Dog" sign can be beneficial as well, even if you don't have a dog.

Detached garages and garden or storage sheds need to be locked and secured. Sheds and garages should have quality locks. Not only are the contents a target for thieves, but tools stored in these structures can be used to burglarize your home. Security for a shed, outbuilding or garage is almost as important as the security for your home.

Trailers of any kind, whether a boat or utility trailer should be secured with a coupler lock to prevent the trailer from being stolen. The keys to the lock should not be kept in the garage.

While it is important for your home to BE secure, it is equally important for your home to LOOK secure. A burglar may choose a target based on what he can see from the street, following the advice in this book can help to make your home BE and LOOK safer.

Key 3 – Do You Know Where Your Keys Are?

Take a minute to think about your keys. In Key 1 we talked about locking your doors. Now that your doors are locked – who has keys?

Many people hide keys to their homes. While this may not be a bad idea from a convenience standpoint, anybody that can find your hidden key can get into your home. Almost any place you can think of to hide a key has also been thought of by a burglar. The first place a burglar will look is under the mat by the front door.

If you do feel you have to hide a key, consider hiding a key at a trusted neighbor's home. If you hide a key at your neighbor's home, a burglar might find the key, but won't know what home the key goes to. Consider installing a keyless lock on at least one door of your home so you don't have to hide a key for those times you are locked out.

Spare home keys and other unused keys need to be stored in a safe, secured, locked place. Avoid keeping important keys on key hooks on the wall in the kitchen. A place where lots of people travel is not a good place to store important keys. If you must, place a key hook inside a cabinet inside a cabinet or pantry. At least it is out of view of visitors in your home.

Replace the exterior door locks when moving into a new home. You never know who still has keys to the home. One alternative is to re-key the existing locks. A locksmith (and some hardware/home improvement stores) can re-key locks for you.

Control your keys. Don't leave your keys unattended, even on your desk at work. Keys are easily duplicated and returned. Keep your keys in a pocket, purse, or anything else worthy of guarding valuables such as credit cards. A person that has your keys has access to everything in your home.

Be careful who you let borrow your keys, whether it's a friend, mechanic or valet. Only hand over the necessary keys, not your whole key-ring.

Don't post pictures of your keys on Twitter, Facebook, or other online service. Keys can be duplicated from photographs. There is currently a website that will duplicate any key that you email them a photo of. Think about that, if someone has only a PHOTO of your key that can be turned into a key.

For your car, if you valet park your car, ALWAYS remove your car key from your key ring and leave ONLY your car key. NEVER leave home keys with a valet or mechanic. Keys are easy to duplicate.

Key 4 – Lighting for Security and Safety

From a security standpoint, few things increase the security of a home as much as lighting. Good lighting is an easy and efficient way to increase your security. Security lighting requires ongoing costs for electricity as well as the cost for initial installation and for bulbs. You can manage lighting costs by using timers and energy efficient lights.

What to Light

The purpose of security lighting is to eliminate places for people to hide. Outdoors, light should be focused around doors, garage doors, carports, patios, walkways and gates. This is often accomplished with decorative porch and wall lights and floodlights. Indoors, lights can be put on timers or photocells to make the home appear occupied.

What Type of Lights

Incandescent and fluorescent lights have been the most common lights in recent years. Incandescent bulbs are cheap, but not energy efficient, and do not last long. Compact fluorescent bulbs (CFL's) have a longer life span than incandescent, and are more energy efficient. Recently, light emitting diode, or LED, lighting designed for the home has become more available. Bulbs fit in existing light sockets and use up to 85% less energy than an incandescent or fluorescent bulb. While an LED bulb is expensive, they last up to 50,000 hours compared to 1,200 hours for an incandescent bulb. You will replace a burned out incandescent bulb *42 times* before an LED bulb fails. The energy savings can be as much as $265 *per bulb*.

Security Light Plan

There are several ways to turn your lights on and off. You can use a switch. You turn the lights on when you need them, and off when you don't. Other options are timers, photocells and motion detectors. Timers turn light on and off at predetermined times, set by you. Photocells turn lights on when it gets dark, and off when it is light. Motion detectors turn lights on when there is movement in front of the light fixture. A combination of different switches is probably best. Use motion detectors outside around doors so you have light when you approach a door. Outdoor security lighting should be mounted high enough to prevent an intruder from breaking or unscrewing a light.

Photocells can be used inside the home turn on lights so that when you never come into a dark home. And lastly, timers can be used to turn lights on and off in a home to make it look like someone is always home. Timers can be set in different rooms to have lights come on and off at various times.

Key 5 – Home Alarm Systems

Do I need an alarm system? Should I get a home alarm system? Excellent questions! Home alarm systems "protect" your home from intruders while you're gone, and can also alert you to intruders while you're home. Home alarm systems may include smoke and fire alarms as well.

A simple home alarm, often called a "burglar alarm," consists of sensors necessary to detect an intrusion, usually door, window, and motion sensors. When a sensor is activated, you are alerted of an alarm by a noise, usually a bell, siren or similar noise. Someone has to hear the alarm, and call the police. A "home security system" includes monitoring of intrusion sensors, fire or smoke sensors, and through security cameras. System monitoring can be through a service, or through "self-service," using the internet and your cell phone.

Monitoring Services

Home alarm systems with monitoring have an initial equipment and installation cost, along with a monthly monitoring fee to your alarm company. "Monitoring" means that someone at a "central station" monitors or watches your system 24 hours a day. The central station monitor calls the police or fire department when the alarm is activated.

If you have your system monitored, there are three ways the system transmits to the central station when an alarm is activated: telephone line, cellular telephone service or internet service. Cellular is safer and more reliable because the alarm system will still function if the telephone lines are cut. Cellular transmission is also faster than a landline connection. Internet transmission sends a signal to the central station through your broadband internet connection. While not as reliable as cellular monitoring, internet transmission is generally less expensive.

Self-Monitoring

Do-it-yourself security systems are available. You can have a simple system that sounds a bell or siren, up to units you can control via your smartphone. There are combination home automation options that also turn on lights and lock/unlock doors.

What happens if I have an intruder? It depends on the type of alarm system you have. A basic system, you get noise. The intruder knows he has been detected, and hopefully leaves. Self-monitored security systems notify you through your cellphone if there is a break in. You would then notify the police or fire departments. A system monitored by a central station will contact you first, and if the alarm company can't reach you, they will notify the police.

Key 6 – Home Camera Systems

Closed circuit camera systems allow you to put cameras in critical areas of your home. Technology allows you to install and use closed circuit television systems (CCTV) to see rooms in your home while you are at home or away. The questions to be answered are: What do you need/want, and how much do you want to spend?

Start with what you really need. Do you want to see video live from a smartphone? How long do you want to save recorded video? Are you going to integrate the video with an alarm system? Do you need low light capabilities? Do you need exceptionally high resolution? Suddenly it seems that there are more questions than answers...

Features

Cost is usually the most important factor for homeowners. Professional installation of a CCTV system costs range from $5,000 and up with a do it yourself system installed for $500 - $1,000. The more security you have (and if you're using video, you probably have a better than average system), the fewer problems you're likely to have.

Useful options include remote viewing and audio. Most systems support some of form of remote viewing (seeing your home when you are not there) over the internet. This is typically done through a smartphone or tablet. Audio monitoring is helpful for people with elderly parents, children or pets. Audio provides a way for homeowners to see and hear what is going on.

Some CCTV systems allow you to see video through your television. This allows you so see what is going on from your bedroom or from anywhere in your home that has a television.

What Do I Want to See?

Your CCTV system should be able to clearly identify people. For example, a camera in a nursery should be focused so you can see movement and activity of an infant. You may want to consider a camera that can change focus – the camera zoomed in on a crib when the child is sleeping and zoomed out when watching the room to monitor a baby sitter. If you are monitoring for intruders, your system should be focused on identifying the person. Fuzzy pictures only let you watch an unidentifiable person take your stuff.

An inexpensive alternative to a complete system is a video doorbell. For less than $200, the Ring Video Doorbell attaches to your front door and sends a video signal to your smartphone. It allows you to look at and talk to anyone standing at your front door from anywhere.

Key 7 – Making Your Home Look Occupied

Statistics show most home burglaries occur in unoccupied dwellings, i.e., when no one is home. One way to prevent a burglary is to make your home LOOK occupied. An intruder will look for an easy target. Anything that you do to make your home look occupied, however small, may be just enough to encourage an intruder to go somewhere else. Make your home look occupied.

Lock all outside doors and windows before you leave the home or go to bed. If you leave home for any reason, even for only a short time, lock your doors. Keep your garage door closed and locked.

Put lights on timers to mimic your typical routine. For example, set a living room timer to go on in the evening for and then set a bedroom light to go on for an hour before your bedtime. Exterior motion lights are effective because you can't sneak up on them, and the sudden light startles intruders, making them think twice about breaking in.

Set a radio on a timer to make it seem like you're there. AM talk radio is best- it sounds like people in the home. Burglars, looking for an empty home, often knock on a front door to see if someone is home, and may leave if they hear a radio.

Change the outside appearance every few days. Lawn chairs on the porch or lawn make a place look occupied. Leave rugs or clothes on a clothes line. Something as easy as moving a flower pot on the porch or a garden hose stretched out in the yard makes a place look occupied. A dog food bowl by the back door can make a potential intruder think twice as well.

If on vacation, have a neighbor change the outside look of the home. Leave a car parked in the driveway (maybe your neighbor's car). Any of these will give the impression people are around. Don't let mail, newspapers or flyers build up while you are away. Arrange with the Post Office to hold your mail, and arrange for a friend to check and collect papers and flyers. Arrange for a neighbor or landscape service to cut your grass if you are going to be away for an extended time. Don't post on social media sites that you are on vacation. You never know when the post could be seen by someone who is not your friend.

Intruders may call your home, and walk up to the door to listen to see if the phone is still ringing. Set your home telephone to off or on the lowest ring setting so strangers won't be able to hear it from outside the home.

Key 8 - Community and Neighborhood Awareness

Go beyond your property line to protect your family and your home. Knowing what is going on in your community and neighborhood allows you to assess what you should be doing and if you should take extra precautions at certain times.

Neighborhood Watch

Neighborhood Watch uses the eyes and ears of you and your neighbors to know what is going on in your neighborhood. If you have a neighborhood association, they may have a Watch group already. If not, step up and get one organized. Your local police department is a good resource for organizing a Neighborhood Watch group. This will also create a line of communication between your neighborhood and the police. Consider inviting local elected officials to attend.

The Neighborhood Watch group will have an initial meeting to organize and learn their duties. You will get to know your neighbors and learn common habits of the neighborhood. General duties are to watch for suspicious behavior such as a car driving slowly through the neighborhood and door knockers. A person going door to door may be handing out religious tracts, looking to work (yardwork or selling) or looking to see who is not home. "Watchers" write down descriptions of persons and vehicles, license plate numbers, and other information that may later identify the person. A police liaison will tell you what to look for and what information is needed for a police response.

Vacation Watch

Some law enforcement agencies provide a service to check your home while on vacation. Check with your local agency to see if they provide such a service. At a minimum, let a trusted friend or neighbor know you are going to be away. Stop your mail and other home deliveries, and arrange to have your grass cut if necessary.

Community Awareness

Watch the local news or read a local newspaper to stay current on community events. You may find community concerns over periodic events such as a local school rivalry and vandalism after the annual football game. Maybe your community has trouble at Halloween or another annual event. This can help you prepare extra precautions during these times. You may want to assess and consider changing your routine if a high profile event is occurring in your community or nationally. Such events often trigger local events nationwide.

Key 9 - In The Event of A Home Invasion

Most of the time, a home invasion occurs when the intruder does not think anyone is home. Most of the time. In the event you are home when an intruder breaks in, you have many options. Here are some suggestions offered by police and personal protection professionals to help you survive a home invasion. Read through all of the suggestions, *and then* make a plan you are comfortable with and feel confident you can carry out.

Quietly exit then call 911 immediately. This gets you out of harm's way. It may not be feasible if other family members are in the home.

Call 911 and lock down in a safe room. Have a code word that alerts family members to go to the safe room. A safe room should have a sturdy door and door frame with a deadbolt lock. If you are building a safe room, consider strengthening interior walls to hinder breaking or shooting through a wall.

Call 911 and scream and make noise. This may scare away the intruder and neighbors may hear your screams.

If Confronted

If you stay and come face to face with the intruders, they may flee. If they do not flee, you have the options of following their orders or defending your and your family. Armed intruders may attack, so knowing what you will do increases your chances of survival. Remember the objective is to survive.

If you choose to defend yourself, what weapons and strategies do you have? Consider taking a self-defense course. Passive resistance suggestions are to make yourself throw up or some other gross action that may startle the intruder and give you time to escape or the intruder to flee. If you are in fear of a sexual assault, telling the intruder you have a sexually transmitted disease may stop the attack.

Weapons and Use of Force

Know the laws in your state on the use of force, both lethal and nonlethal. Many states have passed Stand Your Ground laws to protect you legally if you decide to stay and defend your home.

If you are comfortable using a firearm, use it. The simple display of a firearm may stop the intruder, but you must be prepared if your attacker does not stop. Get training and practice with a firearm. Always secure weapons in a safe place. A good home defense weapon is a pump shotgun. The shotgun projects many pellets versus one bullet from a handgun or rifle. The sound of racking a round in a pump shotgun may be enough to scare away the intruder.

Pepper Spray is a good nonlethal weapon. It is effective and can be used a distance from the intruder. Hand held Tasers are effective, but you must come in reach of the intruder when using, meaning the intruder can grab you. A last resort can be a ball bat, shovel or other object that will disable the intruder. Just pick up a lamp or throw items to discourage attackers.

If your defense comes to hand to hand combat, focus on soft and sensitive areas such as the eyes, ears, nose, and groin. Poke the eyes, punch the nose, box the ears, knee the groin and kick the shins...then stomp on their foot.

Your objective is to stop the threat. You often hear terms such as shoot to kill or strike to maim. Your action is to use the force necessary to stop the intruder. That may cause death or maiming, but the quicker you can stop the threat the quicker the event comes to a close and you and your family is safe.

22 Ricks & Dingle

Key 10 - Computer, Internet and Information Security

Homes today have computers, smartphones and other electronic media capable of being compromised through internet and wireless connections. Lock or log off your computer when you are not using it. Computers (and cellphones) should have passwords to prevent unauthorized entry...even at home. Don't write your username or password on the bottom of your computer or keyboard.

Do not use personal and family names as your password. A hacker will try your name, birthday, address and children's names as passwords. Mix longer passwords with uppercase and lowercase letters with numbers and characters. Passphrases make a long password easy to remember, such as: Ilovemy3childrenEll3nLeslieG@ry.

You should also have passwords for sensitive information stored on your computer like bank records. In the example above, names were spelled using characters to make hacking difficult.

Websites require you to submit your username, along with a password, for identification and security purposes. For high security applications like banking, choose a unique username instead of your email address.

In addition to your computer, wireless routers should have a password to prevent unauthorized users. Hackers will drive slow down streets looking for open wireless access. If they can get on your wireless, they can get on your computer. Change the default name on router and add a complex password. Check printers to see if web services are enabled or disabled – enabled allows hackers to access your home network.

Cloud security and backups

If your computer is stolen, it is easy to get information stored on hard drives in your computer. Not only is the information lost, but information may be compromised. Cloud computing puts your information on a server from an internet company. If your computer is stolen, the only thing the thief gets is your computer.

Virus and malware prevention

Computers are subject to various programs trying to steal your information. Make sure you have some type of program that cleans your computer of unwanted and unnecessary files, and also looks for known spyware, malware and viruses. There are many programs available to protect your computer; some for free as well as some for purchase.

Key 11 - Fire Prevention

By the time you finish reading this chapter, 2 homes will catch fire. The National Fire Protection Association (NFPA) reports there is one home structure fire reported every 86 seconds. Being aware of common ways fires start will reduce the likelihood of your home catching fire.

Cooking

When cooking, stay in the kitchen and keep a safe zone of 3 feet from around the stove. Turn off the stove if you leave the room. Make sure pot handles do not extend off the front of the stovetop where they can be bumped or pulled off. Don't wear loose or baggy clothing that can touch heat sources. Pan fires can usually be smothered by putting a lid on the pan and turning off the burner. Oven fires are usually extinguished by keeping the oven door closed and turning off the heat. Outdoors, place grills out from under eaves, overhanging tree branches, and at least 10 feet from the side of the home.

Open Flame Sources

Fireplaces should be inspected and cleaned annually, and checked monthly for damage. Use a fireplace screen that can stop heavy rolling logs and catch flying sparks. Make sure the fire is out when leaving the home or when going to bed. Collect ashes in an airtight metal container and store outside the home.

Candles should be kept at least 1 foot from anything that can burn. Use sturdy candle holders that won't tip over. Light candles carefully and blow/snuff out candles when leaving the home, leaving the room or going to bed. If you smoke, smoke outside. Extinguish smoking materials in a deep ashtray or a sand filled container.

Douse cigar/cigarette butts and ashes with water before throwing away. Don't toss butts in trash cans. Don't smoke if you are sleepy, have been drinking alcohol, or have taken medicine that makes you drowsy. Never smoke in bed or in a home where oxygen is used, even if the oxygen is not in use.

Electrical Fire Safety

Check appliance cords and plugs. Replace worn or damaged cords. If an appliance has a three- prong plug, do not remove the ground prong (the third prong, usually round) nor try to force a three-prong plug into a two-prong outlet. Don't run cords under rugs or furniture. Do not overload the cord or wall outlet when using extension cords.

Use only appliances evaluated and approved by an organization such as the Underwriters Laboratory (UL). Don't operate major appliances, such as refrigerators, freezers, washers, dryers or air conditioners using extension cords. Use only one heat producing appliance (hair dryer, coffee maker, toaster, space heater, etc.) at a time when plugged into the same receptacle outlet.

Ground-Fault Circuit Interrupter (GFCI) outlets should be installed anywhere that water may be present, such as the kitchen, bathrooms, garage, outdoors, and swimming pools. A qualified electrician should be consulted to assure your home meets local code requirements for GFCI outlets as well as other electrical code requirements. The electrician can also advise you on upgrades for safety, such as Arc-Fault Circuit Interrupters (AFCI). Turn off and replace light switches or outlets that are hot to the touch.

Computers and other electronic media such as your cable or satellite television service are sensitive to electrical surges. These can occur from surges in the powerlines to lighting strikes. Make sure your home electrical system is grounded, and have a good surge protector for all of your electronic components.

Portable Heaters

If your home has areas that need additional heat, consider having stationary heaters installed. If you have portable heaters, use only newer model heaters that are UL approved. Portable heaters should have a thermostat and a tip-over mechanism that will turn the heater off if tipped over. Place heaters away from foot traffic and keep combustible items at least 3 feet away from heaters. Turn off portable heaters when leaving the room or going to bed.

Non-electric heaters using propane, natural gas, or kerosene may give off carbon monoxide. Check local fire codes to see if these types of heaters are approved and any restrictions in their use. Only use the approved fuel for the heater.

Key 12 - Smoke Alarms and Fire Extinguishers

Smoke Alarms

Smoke alarms reduce injury, death and damage from fires. Most homeowners insurance offer discounts for installed smoke and fire alarm systems. There are two main types of alarm: ionized, which responds to flaming fire; and photoelectric, which responds to smoke. It is best to have a combination of both.

Each floor of your home should have a minimum of one alarm. Alarms should be installed in each bedroom and rooms or hallways outside the sleeping area. Place the alarm within 4 inches to 3 feet of the peak of a pitched ceiling. Kitchen alarms should be 10 feet from the stove to minimize false alarms.

Test alarms monthly and replace batteries annually. Newer battery operated alarms have non-replaceable batteries that last 10 years. When the low battery alert sounds (usually a periodic beep), you just replace the whole unit. Some alarms can be interconnected which allows all alarms to sound if smoke is detected at one alarm. There are also models with strobes to alert deaf or hard of hearing occupants.

Fire Alarms

Home alarm companies offer a fire alarm that alerts the fire department. Advanced features include notifying you of a fire on your smartphone, unlocking doors for fire department access, and turning off power.

Carbon Monoxide Alarms

Carbon monoxide (CO) alarms alert you to dangerous CO levels. There are combination smoke and CO alarms, but you can get CO only alarms. These alarms act alike and can be interconnected like a smoke only alarm, and can be monitored by home alarm systems. While a smoke alarm usually gives off steady beeps, CO alarms give off intermittent beeps-usually 4 beeps, pause, 4 beeps. They should be installed at the same locations as fire alarms.

Fire Extinguishers

Portable fire extinguishers are useful with small fires, usually in a small area and not growing, such as a kitchen fire or trash can. Home extinguishers should be multi-purpose, meaning they can be used on common home fires. Select one that is large enough to handle a small fire, but easy for you to handle. Place extinguishers close to an exit and keep your back clear for easy exit. They should be used only after everyone has evacuated the building and the room is not filled with smoke. Call the fire department.

Fire departments and fire extinguisher companies provide the best training on using extinguishers. Until you can attend this training, read all instructions and search the internet for videos showing you how to use an extinguisher. When using an extinguisher, remember PASS:

Pull the pin and point the nozzle away from you.
Aim low, pointing the extinguisher at the base of the fire.
Squeeze the lever to dispense the extinguisher.
Sweep the nozzle from side to side at the base of the fire.

Even if you think the fire is out, the fire department should check to assure the area is safe. Do not reenter your home until it is safe to do so.

After a Fire

It may be that you will need to go elsewhere after a fire. If safe to enter the home, gather valuables and go to an alternate location. You may need to board up the home to prevent looting while the home is unoccupied. Contact your insurance provider so they can start the process of getting your home back in order. Inventory your valuables, furniture and belongings for insurance claims. Take pictures of high value items and make sure you have enough coverage for fire damage for those items.

Key 13 - Fire Evacuation Plan

Have a plan on what you will do in a fire. Test the plan and work out any problems before going over the plan with the family. Then have a drill!

Start with a map of each floor of your home that shows all doors and windows. Have two ways out of each room. If a way out is through a window, make sure the window opens easily. The area around doors and windows should be clear of furniture or items that may delay your exit. Consider what you will need for persons who need assistance and also pets. Once out of the home, have a place where the family will meet such as a mailbox or street light.

If a window is to be used as an escape is a far distance from the ground, an emergency ladder can be placed by the window. Emergency ladders have instructions on the ladder, but it is best to practice deploying the ladder before and during family fire drills. If you decide to practice climbing down the ladder, start with a low elevation such as a first floor window and use safety precautions to prevent an injury during practice.

The Plan

With your family, go over the plan with everybody knowing how to get out of each room in the home. Practice as if there was a real fire. Do a complete walkthrough, always ending up at the meeting spot. No one reenters the home until all have met at the meeting spot and an adult has announced it safe to go inside the home.

Then drill! Really drill! Be as realistic as possible. Have noise and create confusion during the exit so all will know how to react under stress.

When There is a Fire

When the alarm sounds or someone tells you there is a fire, leave immediately. Everyone call 911 to make sure the fire department is notified. Take the safest route out of the home. Touch doors before opening. If the door is warm to the touch, consider the alternate exit. A last resort is to stay in the room with the door closed. Place a towel or sheets under the door and call the fire department to tell them your location. If you cannot call, go to a window so you can signal your location. A flashlight or bright cloth is helpful in signaling. Go to the meeting place. Do not go back in the home until the fire department says it is safe.

Key 14 - Disaster and Emergency Planning

What potential natural or manmade events may cause a major disaster in your area? Hurricane? Earthquake? Blizzard? Most communities have an emergency preparedness office that can provide you with detailed information on the disasters to prepare for. Be prepared to be without utilities, phone service, etc. for several days.

Before a Disaster

Start with having an emergency radio or smartphone app that alerts you to bad weather or other hazardous conditions. It is good to purchase a battery operated radio you can use during an emergency. Cell phone services are often restricted to emergency personnel with special access codes during an emergency. Monitor daily weather reports from local news stations to be aware of developing conditions that may cause a disaster. The time between notification of an event and the event will be spent preparing for what you will do.

Have 1 gallon of water per person per day and non-perishable food. Plan on a 3 day supply if you will evacuate the area, and 2 weeks supply for sheltering at home. Remember food for your pets. Keep at least a 1 week supply of all medications you need. In addition to a battery operated radio, have a flashlight and extra batteries for both.

Other helpful items are books and games for children, a first aid kit, a manual can opener, disinfectant, tools, duct tape and plastic sheeting.

During a Disaster

In most events, you will shelter at home. If a tornado is pending, shelter in a basement or interior room on the lowest level of the home. In a winter storm, be prepared to close off rooms and stay in one room to stay warm. Use caution with emergency generators; make sure they are away from the home and the generator does not exhaust in the home or under the eaves of the home.

If an event causes contaminated air, you may be advised to shelter in place by placing plastic sheeting over doors and windows to seal all gaps that allow air to enter. Turn off air conditioners, heaters and vents.

If you must evacuate for a disaster, have a kit ready that contains your important documents.

Key 15 - Personal Safety

There is not a creep behind every rock, but there are some out there, and being aware of your surroundings increases your safety. The person who followed you out of the store and down the same lane where you parked may just be looking for their car too.

Have 360° Awareness

Become a hard target. When driving, walking through a parking garage or parking lot, or walking down the street, watch what is going on around you. Don't get distracted by your smart phone or fumbling for your keys. Look at people around you.

Soft targets don't watch their surroundings. You are leaving the mall after holiday shopping. You are thinking about all your packages you are juggling to your car. Periodically take packages out to your vehicle. Shop with a friend. Ask store or mall security to escort you to your vehicle.

I Think I am Being Followed

First, don't show you are afraid. By reading this, you are developing knowledge and skill that will increase your safety. Have your cell phone ready. If you don't have a weapon (firearm, pepper spray, etc.) think of what you may have that can be a weapon: keys, pens, etc. Keys placed alternately between your fingers can be raked across an assailants face to distract and injure them. Remember, your objective is to stay safe and protect yourself.

Stay on main streets where others are present to see and help if necessary. Try crossing the street and walking in the opposite direction to see if the person follows. Step into a store or restaurant and see what they do. If they walk in, walk out. If they walk out, go back in and tell someone you are being followed. Call the police.

Tell the person in a loud voice to stop following you. Be clear and specific as to what you want the person to do. Screaming draws little attention, but yelling, "Take your hands off of me!" makes people look to see what is happening.

If you get caught down a secluded street or parking lot, act like you know what you are doing and move to main streets where people are. If necessary, run to put distance between you and your attacker. If the begin to pursue you, you are being attacked. Taking defensive action would be considered necessary to prevent injury to you.

Key 16 – Driving Safety

Local travel routines are usually not a problem, but high profile executives, government officials, and celebrities benefit by changing routines to avoid being followed. Stalkers may follow you from work, the store, gym and other places you frequent. It is a good idea to know different routes to and from your home so you will be prepared for unexpected events.

The Unpredictable "Routine"

If you feel a need to prevent your being followed, make your "routine" unpredictable. Drive a different way to and from work every day. Change your departure and arrival times to confuse possible stalkers. Do the same when going to the gym, store, bank, etc. Change days, times, and vehicles. Take your spouse's car once in a while. Take your spouse or a friend with you. Anything to mix up the routine.

I Think I am Being Followed

If you think you are being followed, don't go home. Stay on the main streets. Stop and see if the vehicle passes you. If they stop, drive off. Another tactic is to make four right turns and see if the vehicle you think is following you does the same. If so, it is very likely you are being followed. Stay on the main streets and call the police, or go to a convenient store or gas station. This would be someplace you can quickly get out of your car and into the store. Tell store attendants what is going on and ask them to call the police. If possible, record license plate numbers.

Key 17 - Children and Neighborhood Security

Does your child walk to school, or leave/return home alone? If so, there are some steps to take that will make them safer. These principals also apply when they are playing in the neighborhood or going to the park or other outside activities.

Have a Cell Phone

Every child wants one, and this is a good reason for them to have one. Make sure the phone you purchase has the ability to let you track and monitor your child's whereabouts. There are specific apps that let you track their location as well as monitor or block unwanted cell phone activity.

While leaving/arriving and even walking home, your child can call you to let you know they are safe. You can call and check on them while they are playing or at a friend's home.

Let Trusted Neighbors Know

A trusted neighbor will know what time your child is expected to leave or return from school and can look out for them. If there is an event, your child will know where to go first if they need help.

Don't Take Shortcuts

Tell children that walk to school, park, club or running errands not to take shortcuts. This can be a cut through a person's yard, through a wooded area, or behind a store, carwash, etc. Tell your child to stay on the sidewalks and main streets when going to and from activities.

Strangers Approaching

If a stranger approaches, tell your child to run to a trusted neighbor or friend. If the stranger is in a car, do not approach the car. A ploy is for a person to ask a child to help find a lost dog and ask the child to get in the car and ride around to look for the lost pet.

Other ploys are to offer a ride to school, candy, money or drugs. All are attempts to get the child close enough for the person to grab them. Let your child know it is important to let you know if this occurs even if they think it is nothing. Report all incidents to your local police.

Strangers Posing as Police Officers

A rare occurrence is for a stranger to pose as a police officer and demand your child go with them. This usually occurs with a person in plainclothes posing as a detective, but fake uniforms have been used. A real police officer will understand the concern of a child who wants to call his or her parents to address their concern. The child may go to the trusted neighbor for assistance. Show your child the uniforms of local police. Most departments have pictures of uniforms and badges on their websites.

Have a Code Word

A child may go with a person if told there is a family emergency. While your child should never go with a stranger, it may be necessary for a friend or distant family member (someone who does not live with you) to pick up the child. Have a code word that you and your child know and give it to the person. The child should ask for the code word if the adult does not give the word when picking them up.

Key 18 – What You Need to Know About Your Child's School

If you have children attending school, get to know the teacher and administrators. This develops a relationship that will promote the welfare of your child. Getting involved with the school promotes the safety of your child and creates a positive learning environment.

Register who is authorized to pick up your child. Make sure the school will notify you immediately if someone not on the list tries to pick up your child. This is also the time to advise the school on the use of your child's name and photograph in the media or school events. It is best NOT to allow the school to use photographs or names. Never give blanket permission to use personal information.

Find out if there is a school nurse and what the procedures are for sending medications to school with your child. What will the school do if there is a medical emergency and you are not available for consent? Look at the options the school offers and decide on a plan that satisfies you.

Emergency plans

Schools are trained to handle a multitude of emergencies. The plans should be in a student handbook or on the school website. If not, ask for a copy. During an emergency, follow the school plans. Parents wanting to step in during an emergency may make matters worse. For example, cars blocking school entrances may prevent emergency vehicles from entering or exiting the school as well as possibly putting the parent in harm's way. Learn the schools Family Reunification Plan on how they will inform families of an incident and the steps in the reunification process.

Make sure the emergency plan covers: shelter in place, lockdowns, active shooter, severe weather, evacuation, accounting for all persons after an event, and steps for when a student is unaccounted for.

Off campus activities

What procedures does the school follow when taking students off campus for field trips and activities such as sporting events? How many adults will be available? Is there a procedure if a parent decides to sign their child out during or at the end of an off campus event? Are parent chaperones screened?

Bullying and Other Threats

Bullying can be physical or psychological and threatens another in many ways. Some warnings your child may be bullied are: torn clothing, unexplained cuts and bruises, lost items (hats, books, etc.) a change in mood and demeanor, and makes excuses for not wanting to go to school. Know the school policy for addressing bullying. Also, know the signs your child may be bullying others: becomes aggressive, gets into fights, has friends who bully, is sent to the principal or detention often, has unexplained money or items, and denies responsibility, usually blaming others for their problems. Report any incidents of bullying or suspected bullying to school officials.

The school should be notified if you are aware of threats made by a student or other person regarding the school. Schools have personnel trained to analyze and assess conditions to take steps to prevent a tragedy.

Key

Checklists

Key A- Home Security Checklist

How many people live here?

Who has keys/access to the home?

> Keys
>
> Garage Door opener
>
> Access Codes

Do you have an inventory of your assets (furniture, jewelry, weapons, tools, etc.) and its value in priority order?

Check Insurance coverage: Fire, theft, personal injury, business loss, etc.

General appearance of the home:

> Vegetation close to buildings, obstructing view
>
> Clean, orderly or unkempt
>
> Visible deterrent: Sign noting alarm in use

Is there a plan for home security?

> Saferoom – wall construction, door and lock meets external standards

Is there a plan in the event of a home invasion?

Is there a plan for fires and evacuation?

Are critical assets secured in high security containers?

What is the fire rating on this container?

Are all important papers shredded before discarding?

What are the physical boundaries of the yard?

Is there a fence?

Is the fence strong and in good repair?

Are gates solid and in good condition?

Are gates locked?

Are entrances well lit?

Are exterior doors solid wood or metal, and 1 ¾" thick?

Are exterior door frames secured to the house frame?

Are door hinge pins located on the inside?

Are door hinges installed so that it would be difficult to remove the door(s)?

Are the exterior locks double cylinder, dead-bolts, or jimmy-proof type locks?

Do all locks work properly?

Can the breaking of glass or a door panel allow someone to open the door from the outside?

Is this glass protected by security glazing, a security screen or bars?

Do padlocks, chains, and hasps meet minimum security standards?

Are the hasps installed so that the screws/bolts cannot be removed?

Do windows that open have locks that can be opened by breaking the glass?

Are windows protected by security glazing, a security screen or bars?

Can windows be removed without breaking them?

Are vents and utility access having a gross area of one square foot or more secured with protective coverings (door, grate, etc.)?

Is the outdoor area lighted? Yard, doors, garage, utiltity buildings

During what hours is lighting used? (dusk to dawn or timer)

Are light fixtures vandal proof? (i.e., unscrewing of bulbs)?

Is the wiring high enough to reduce tampering?

Is there alternate or emergency power for the lighting system?

Is lighting sufficient for CCTV?

Is there an alarm system?

Type of Sensors: Microwave, Passive Infrared, or Mechanical switch

Who monitors? Homeowner or central station (how is it connected)

Who responds to alarms? Homeowner, police, or Guard Service

Is the system tamper resistant?

Is there an alternate, or independent, source of power in the event of power Failure?

Is this home monitored with Closed Circuit Television?

Who monitors? (Usually the homeowner)

Does the alarm company have access to cameras?

Are events recorded (constant or motion detection)?

Where are cameras located (overt, covert)

Cameras in use: B&W Color Infrared PTZ Wireless RF

Key B – Fire Safety Checklist

Taken from USFA.FEMA.gov

Smoke alarms on each level of the home

Smoke alarms inside and outside sleeping areas

Smoke alarms tested monthly

All residents (especially children) know the sound of an alarm

You have a fire escape plan

You practice the fire escape plan

Carbon Monoxide alarms on each level of the home

Ignitable materials out of reach of children

Electrical cords in good condition

Dryer is cleaned of lint after each use

Candles are in/on sturdy containers that will not tip over

Candles are extinguished when going to bed or leaving the home

Flammable liquids are kept in approved containers

Oily cloths are kept in proper containers
Items cooked are constantly attended by someone in the kitchen
Pot handles turned to back of stove
Fire extinguisher is in a conspicuous place
No open flames if oxygen is in use in the home
Have furnaces inspected at the beginning of each heating season
Use only approved space heaters
Turn space heaters off when going to bed and when leaving the home
Firepits and grills should be 3 feet from the home
Ourdoor fires should be constantly monitored
Make sure outdoor fires are out before leaving

Key C – Home Inventory

For insurance and theft reports, identify valuable assets and record them for verification of ownership. Photograph items and record serial numbers or other identifying information. Have unusually expensive items appraised and make sure your homeowners policy fully covers such losses.

Jewelry

Art

Collectibles (figurines)

Electronics

> Televisions/Monitors
>
> DVD/DVR/Cable/Satellite box
>
> Gaming systems
>
> Stereos/speakers
>
> Computers
>
> Telephones, including cellphones

Kitchen

> Major appliances – Stove, Refrigerator, Freezer
>> Freezer contents
>
> Washer/dryer
>
> Small appliances- microwave, coffeemaker
>
> Silver flatware and silver service
>
> Crystal and china
>
> Wine/liquor

Tools

> Power tools- drill, saws,
>
> Hand tools- wrenches, socket sets
>
> Gas power tools- chainsaw, weedeater, blower
>
> Mower and attachments
>
> Yard tools- shovels, rakes

Hobby Supplies

Guns and other weapons

Musical Instruments

Exercise equipment

Outdoor furniture

    Lawn and patio chairs and tables

    Swings/gliders/rockers

    Grill

    Hot tub

    Pool and accessories (pumps and other gear)

Recreation

    RV- camper or motorhome

        RV Contents

    Boat

    ATV

    Trailer

Furniture

    Chairs/sofa

    Tables

    Wall pictures/wall hangings

        Tapestries

        Animal mounts

Bedroom- bed, dresser

Bathroom accessories

Clothes and shoes

Rugs

Linens and towels

Key D – Disaster and Emergency Plan Checklist

Taken From FEMA.gov:

Portable battery powered radio with extra batteries

Weather radio

Flashlight and extra batteries

Matches in a waterproof container

Tools

> Shut off wrench or pliers for gas/water disconnect
>
> Hammer
>
> Shovel
>
> Screwdrivers

Potable water

Easy to prepare foods (camping food stores well)

Special needs food

Kitchen utensils (manual can opener, pan, knive, etc.)

Plates, napkins, etc.

60 Ricks & Dingle

Plastic sheeting
Duct tape
Work gloves
First aid kit
Prescription medicines
Over counter medications
Antiseptic and disinfectants
Sunscreen
Soap
Washcloths
Towels
Other personal hygiene items
Change of clothes
Cold weather gear
Sunglasses
Sunblock
Bedding supplies (sheets, blankets, etc.)
Driver's license/passport
Cash
Credit cards
Extra house/car keys

Personal documents: (Birth Certificate, Social
Security Cards, insurance papers, bank account
information, etc.)

Maps (GPS and cell phones may not work)

For More Information:

Check out these organizations and websites

Stopbullying.gov

Ready.gov

Consumer Product Safety Commission: www.cpsc.gov

energy.gov

redcross.org

fema.gov

National Crime Prevention Council: www.ncpc.org

About the Authors

Bobby Ricks has written two previous books on Physical Security: Physical Security and Safety; and Security Management. He is a Certified Protection Professional (CPP) through ASIS International. Bobby graduated with a B.S. in Police Administration (with Distinction) from Eastern Kentucky University and a Juris Doctorate from the University of Memphis. His security experience includes the U.S. Air Force Security Police, Director of the Office of Crime Prevention for the Richmond, Kentucky Police Department, the Federal Bureau of Investigation, the Federal Law Enforcement Training Center, and Lockmasters.

Jeff Dingle has written numerous articles and a previous book on Physical Security: Physical Security and Safety. He is a Certified Protection Professional (CPP) through ASIS International. Jeff graduated with a Bachelor's degree in Criminology from Florida State University. Jeff's physical security experience includes the Office of Security for the National Security Agency, the Federal Law Enforcement Training Center, the Carter Presidential Library, Home Depot, Lockmasters, and PCI Gaming.

www.ingramcontent.com/pod-product-compliance
Lightning Source LLC
Chambersburg PA
CBHW022130280326
41933CB00007B/624